FINISHING LINE PRESS

www.finishinglinepress.com

The Scar It Leaves

poems by

Charley Allen-Dunn

Finishing Line Press
Georgetown, Kentucky

The Scar It Leaves

ACKNOWLEDGMENTS

I am forever grateful for the support and inspiration of Mr. Bob Head. Thank
you for taking me on walks through the woods and helping me believe I
have something worth saying.

Thank you to my cousin, Jana Duffy, for loving me wholly and
unconditionally. I am always in awe of your bravery and fight for the people
you love.

Lastly, to Kala — thank you for your encouragement, copy-editing, and,
most of all, love. Thank you for always listening when I read the same things
over and over and for believing in me when I thought I would never get
things right.

Publisher: Leah Huete de Maines
Editor: Christen Kincaid
Cover Art: Robert William Head,
          Old Growth, Amputation, New Growth, ...Tofino, Pacific Rim....,
          5' x 6', Oil on Canvas
Author Photo: Robyn Pizzo
Cover Design: Elizabeth Maines McCleavy

Order online: www.finishinglinepress.com
          also available on amazon.com

Author inquiries and mail orders:
Finishing Line Press
PO Box 1626
Georgetown, Kentucky 40324
USA

Contents

Until it pops 1

The gradual onset of chemical dependence 2

At what point do you stop reaching for the flame? 6

Enough just to know 8

In all that time, it never occurred to me to cushion the fall 10

There's a poem in this place 12

Before/After 13

Until there is nothing left to forget 14

And everything was still 16

After the thaw 17

In the quiet 18

Top of the world 19

Never stop saying her name 20

Grace, unspoken 22

I would follow you anywhere 23

Until it pops

As children, we filled our lungs with air
and blew as hard as we could,
powdery rubber turned wet
between our lips.

It built like a movement —
the soft stirring of woodwinds
before the stampede of percussion,
the shriek of the strings,
the sudden crash of the cymbal.

What I learned to hate the most was the build-up,
the steady flow of breath
that stretched the air
until it shimmered —
the tightness in the chest of knowing
before you know.

The wolf's breath on your neck,
the slick skid on black ice,
the lipstick on the collar.

Over time, we get better at picking up the pieces,
we learn where the remnants of latex land
when they explode.

Even then, we never learn to stop.
We pucker our lips all the faster,
and begin to blow.

The gradual onset of chemical dependence

I.

My brother sets forest fires at the kitchen table,
blowing embers best left forgotten
into roaring walls of flame.
We flinch back, seeking refuge against the walls, but
not him. He flails in growing circles —
a top spinning,
fiercely burning,
and only just starting to tilt.

II.

His partner drives him up for the day,
his words slur, his cheeks droop under
eyes that look like pieces of charcoal dropped in puddles
of the cherry kool-aid we drank in hot Kentucky summers.

My sister said he was better last time —
not himself, but able to hold a conversation
without pauses that stretched across the room
like a dense, heavy fog.
Today, his shoulders droop
under the weight of the head his neck
has given up holding.

He is always on the verge of nodding off.

This morning, he'd walked into our parents' house
where he stumbled and sat, falling into faded leather,
a marionette with broken strings.

My mother's eyes met mine
and we looked away.
Ashamed.

We have slowly started to accept that boy we knew
was lost somewhere last fall.

It seemed so sudden —
a few rambling phone calls in September,
messages left unanswered in October,
a Thanksgiving of unending speeches replacing conversation.
A Christmas of slurred words and clumsy hands.

Slowly and all at once —
the brother I knew fading further
with every visit.

III.

The August grass turned to dust in the drought.
Your surgeon said he could fuse two vertebrae —
no more pain. No more pills.
A wave of the wand,
a simple slice of the scalpel,
a miracle of modern medicine.

And it worked.

For a season, we had you —

clear-eyed and listening, speaking, conversing.
But still, not you. Your words clipped through clenched jaws —
angry, bitter. A summer storm,
the crack of guilt, the sharp slash of fury.

After sleepwalking through years, you'd woken to find
a stranger — aged, overweight, thinning hair. A partner
who stayed but a reminder, constant
of the things you will never remember,
refuse to remember saying and doing.

Gusts of wind scatter us to the corners
of the room when you walk in.
Squirrels chattering in treetops.
Everyone always on guard.

And then
the pain came back
inevitable as the bitter cold of winter.
Headaches like ice picks and you went
to the ER for comfort but they looked
at your chart and marked you —
drug-seeker. An addict. A phony. A fake.

Your surgeon said the surgery had been a success
but now, the discs above and below. A shaky foundation,
trusses bowing and beginning to split.

Another surgery inevitable,
but first — physical therapy.
Injections. Steroids. And drugs,
drugs, so many drugs. The habit
you fought so hard to kick,
a reunion tour, a reprieve
from that cold harsh light you'd woken up to.

Like swimming in the ocean in winter, you forget
how cold the wind will be when you surface. The air stings
as it fills your lungs, your eyes squint against salt-spray
so you slip back. Under the water,
your limbs feel heavy, warm.
Relief wraps around you like a flannel blanket,
comfort seeps through your skin
all the way to the bone.
Everything becomes easy,
simple, until it is too late
to resist when you realize

all this time,
you've been sinking
like a stone.

At what point do you stop reaching for the flame?

One of the first words the children in my family learn is "hot."
Point to the steam rising from the cup — hot,
point to the stove glowing angry red — hot,
sausages sizzling on sticks — hot,
candles dripping wax on the cake just before we start to sing — hot.

Hot. HhhhhhoT.
Drag it out,
blow into the h,
let it breath and spread,
then a quick ah and clip.
Stop hard with the T.

HhhhhhhhoT

Let the h rumble like the purr of a motor,
puff your cheeks around the o at 10 and 2,
now slam the brakes. Throw your arm out.

T

Let the h build like the heat as you move your hand closer,
warmer, warmer, then touch it. The sharp inhale,
the rapid recoil of the T.

A blister already beginning to bubble. We feel the heat,
we grow to expect the burn, we learn and remember
the sharp sting that doesn't fade for days.
The scar it leaves.

But, still, we light the match. We gather our kindling
and blow gently, smile as it catches, watch it build,
build,
build,
build until
it snatches the air from our lungs. Dancing, swaying,

crackling, beckoning, devouring,
luring us in until
the only thing left is ash.

Enough just to know

My brother texts to say
his partner of twenty years is leaving
"just so you hear it from me"

"Just so you hear it from me"
just seven words for twenty years
and the space between each one filled
with exasperation, flippancy.

As if we are both on separate mountains
searching across the valley to see
lights twinkle on the horizon,
satiated and safe in knowing
the other still breathes.

No pull to call out, to speak, to sing
voices echoing, layering, sound waves
cresting, creating a rip tide, working together
to make the ocean push-pull dance
across the sand.

The blood we share, decades and years —
Saturday mornings spent kneeling in front of cartoons,
the imprint of carpet on our knees, Christmas mornings
when you tip-toed into my room beaming, winking
incapable of saying Santa forgot without laughing. Or the morning,
after your dog died when I woke to find you curled
at the end of the bed.
Or the nights we try to forget — our father's anger
roaring and burning everything in its path
but always, especially you.

The night I came home from college
and you took me out to talk. We'd made it home,
headlights reflecting in the side door glass, when I finally
found the words to say I was gay. The way you slipped
the gear into reverse, and we sped away again.

We drove for hours down backroads and sideroads, dead-ends
and highways, talking. Your hand always on my shoulder,
squeezing when I cried. And you never lied.
You never said it would be easy, but you said
you would be there. And you were.

You were always there
until you weren't.

In all that time, it never occurred to me to cushion the fall

When I was ten, my friend had a treehouse,
perched up high with a ladder that went
straight up and like Jack on the beanstalk,
I climbed.

I remember it twenty, forty, fifty feet high and I
went up and up.
I curled my arms around each rung,
knees wobbling, scraping my forearms with splinters,
before settling my feet
to start again.

At the top, I peeked over the edge —
super soakers, GI Joes, a football
a world built for the boys who never thought
I could make the climb.
I placed my hands on the side with pride,
so sure of the last few rungs, I never looked.

I fell in slow motion,
a camera zooming out,
the fade of the treehouse, the branches,
the open mouths of the boys overhead.

Hitting the ground was like hitting play —
everything there all at once — my back in the dirt,
ribs shifting like an earthquake, the air
whooshing out of my lungs.

There are moments now when I still feel that same ache in my chest —
cleaning the house, telling a joke, walking the dogs,
washing my hands before breakfast.
And I feel it — the sudden shock, the chest quake, the whoosh of air,
the stunned silence and sting of tears.

Someday, before we're ready,
we will bury my brother.

After I fell, I dug my fingers into the dirt
and lay looking at the ladder.
Knowing what happened and how but still, somehow, not sure.

There's a poem in this place

There's a poem in this place
where the crops roll green into the tree line,
where the ghost of a city rests beneath the lake,
where the storms take houses down past the studs,
where the factories shut down,
where the lightning cracks like a whip,
where the trees twist and turn around barbed wire,
where the people who leave don't come back,
where the people who stay wear the past like shackles to their feet

There's a poem in this place
where we grew up in shadows,
where the gospel bloomed like ragweed,
where the secrets sprouted like dandelions,
where the whispers always came after the smile,
where we learned loving wasn't always right

There's a poem in this place,
where the sky some days is a blue so pure it makes you forget,
where the sun sets so red-orange-purple it takes your breath to see it,
makes you want to reach out your hand to share it
but still believe it was meant only for you.

Before/After

We mark time in befores and afters —
moments when everything changed but, still
the after becomes the same, routine, until something else —
the car wreck, the marriage, the baby,
the thing that broke you — almost,
or the thing that made the breath catch in your chest — joy,
pure and plain, filling you up to the point
where you could burst,
but you don't.

We think we'll never survive it,
but we do. It fades like the couch you've had since college,
like the dark of your hair,
like the scar from your first time falling,
so slow you hardly notice —
and then — just there.

We think we'll never forget
the magic of the first kiss,
the electric charge from her fingertips,
the way our bodies burned when we touched, but time
softens the edges,
softens our bellies,
blurs what we see until
we barely see each other.

Until there is nothing left to forget

In a village, once,
a family in a cave,
the pup they raised, genial and kind,
grew rabid in old age.

They held the cure to his lip,
but lock-jawed and hackles raised,
he snarled and snapped away.

He ran loose through the country —
ravaging, savaging, snarling.
The family concerned but safe
in their cave.

They forgot.

Every so often, the beast would
venture home, head hung low
and hurting. They cried, nursed his wounds
and, as he healed, his hackles raised
again. Again, they held the cure
to his locked jaws, again,
he snarled, snapped, and broke away.

The family would stand at the edge of the sunlight,
the cure secured in a pocket,
and survey the savagery,
lament the state of the land.

"What can we do?"
they sang in chorus.
"What can we do?"
as they patted the pocket with the cure,
kicked aside ropes and chains
and scurried back into the shadows.

They forgot.
The beast returned with blood
still fresh on his lips, a body half gone
left at the edge of the dark,
where he limped deeper into the fading light.

The family rejoiced — their pup come home —
another chance, assured that this time
his lips would part for the cure.

They nursed his wounds, washed his matted fur,
massaged his paws and yet, again,
as the wounds closed, as his strength returned,
his hackles began to raise.

He watched them pat their pockets
contemplating, and, again, he locked his jaws.
Again, he snapped and snarled.
Again, he broke away.

Again, the family stood at the edge of the sunlight,
singing their song of lament
as they surveyed the savagery,
before sinking back into the darkness.

They forgot.

And everything was still

The space between here and there,
floating in limbo, the will they, the won't they.
The after, but still before —
the feather lifting to float on the wind
before it reaches the ground and stills.

The inhale, so deep, of her smell
before the breath leaves your lungs.

The feel of her name in your mouth
before the last letter, the smile, slips from your lips.

The life you lived, the romance, the laughter but now

the soft of her skin, her hand, still warm,
the squeeze before her fingers slip.

After the thaw

The crocus push their heads through soil
like soldiers on lookout.
February's gray turned to March's kelly green.
Not a blockbuster in technicolor,
but indie-arthouse mumblecore,
subtle and steady.
The sky that blue we always seem to forget —
every shade at once, an ocean flipped overhead.

Wind like warm waves soothes the sting
from winter's sharp knife slashes,
carries away the remnants of fall when
words crumbled like autumn leaves between my lips.

Too many promises sworn and broken
underneath heavy clouds spitting sleet and snow. Too many
not nows, not agains, never knowing whens,
trapped in nights that seemed to never end.

Sunlight filters through branches just beginning to bud and bloom,
I lift my head to feel my cheeks warm and stay silent.

Our shoulders brush when we walk.
I stumble from sideways smiles,

our fingers brush, flit,
a monarch pausing on forsythia.

You wink. A seed just beginning to sprout.

In the quiet

Afternoon light filters through the window glass,
lighting up dust like plankton at the bottom of the sea
as it filters and floats
to settle at the small of your back.
Blankets pushed low to your hips,
I brush my fingertips down the mountains and valleys
of your spine.

Soft skin, strong muscle,
grown stronger in the weeks we didn't speak.

I used to dream we were underwater.
Your hair grown long, tangled
like seaweed amidst the coral.
Light casting your face
half in shadow.

Your eyes open wide beneath the waves,
hands rippling water,
fingers pointing,
words lost in bubbles and rising
to the surface
to burst.

With shaky sea legs, we spent weeks
dancing — two steps forward, three steps back,
a shuffle to the side. We circled in orbit,
shifting slowly closer with every turn until
the impossible, the inevitable,
the unexpected impact.

I brush your hair behind your ear,
your lips curve in a smile as you sleep,
shifting closer still.

Top of the world

At dawn, the sun hides somewhere behind a humid haze,
viscous, thick, like layers of paint on panes of glass,
and we climb hills like sandy mountains —
up and up and still further up,
so I high I teeter on tiptoes
and strain to catch a glimpse
of a sailboat as it slip-slides shimmies
just over the horizon.

Chests heaving,
sweat staining our shirt collars,
we reach the top
and look out to find an artist's palette
spread beneath us. Blue in every shade —
carolina, cornflower, sapphire, electric.
Wildflower mounds of gesso golds and hills
that roll like sound travels
in emerald, army, kelly greens.

A winding, bending, curling, twisting
labyrinth of tans and taupes and browns
mark the trails we could have traveled.

Choices right or wrong,
decisions — deliberate and happenstance,
some circumstance but still —
no map, no compass, no markers —
still, somehow, we found a path
that led us here.
This spot so high we can see the sun
begin to blaze brighter,
watch as it unravels the fog, burning frayed edges,
until the only things left are shimmers of light, heat
and the sparking salt of the Pacific
turned sweet on your sun-drenched skin.

Never stop saying her name

We stretch out on the deck in frayed lawn chairs,
small with fold-up metal frames. The kind I recognize
from old photographs — frozen smiles on hot summer days.

The deck is weathered, gray,
but sturdy, strong. No railing
lest it obstruct the view —
tall trees, a carpet of moss, birds fighting over hot pepper suet.

He reads us a poem and talks about African folklore,
how, in some places, the grieving would cut a hole
in the side of the house
instead of taking their dead through the door.
They kept shrines, artifacts, places of honor
to remember the "living dead," the spirit
that never truly dies until the death
of the last person who remembers.

Saying their names kept the spirits close.
Kept them near. Home. Safe.

He says Nita's name instead of saying "my wife." He keeps
her clothes hung still in the closet,
books stacked and untouched on the nightstand.
In my wife, he sees something that gives him hope
that she might carry the memory
when he no longer can.

He gives her skirts, dresses, scarves.
She slips away to the bathroom to try them on.
When he claps, as she twirls, his face
appears as it must have then. Delight,
for a moment, erasing decades.

I watch her, too, and think
how the unlucky but loved always end up here,
how one of us will, too.

The pressure of surviving, the fear
of failing, forgetting, of misplacing
photographs or tossing out knickknacks — the things
she kept but never told you why. The things you keep
but meaning lost except
they meant something to her once,
something you'll never know.

Grace, unspoken

After the brake slam —
after the sudden cinching of the seat belt —

after the record scratch squeal of tires,
after the jaw-clenching, teeth-gritting, arm-bracing,
whole-body-tensing, sudden

stop

inches
from an impact
that never comes,

the deer will glance, just once,
before it disappears
into the woods.

I would follow you anywhere

In March, he knows the lady slippers will suddenly stretch past the earth and raise their arms to the sun. Every day, he walks the path through the woods, winding his way through the trees. Cataloging. Checking. Christmas fern fronds and Jacob's ladder. Wild ginger and black cohosh. Marking the spot so next year he'll know where to look for the turkscap lily, the virginia bluebell when spring starts to stir.

Decades ago, they held hands and walked the drive he'd cleared. Together, they imagined their future — a garden here, a stone path, a house with room to breathe and windows to watch the sun rise and set and the birds swoop through the sky while they lingered over coffee. Later, they both knelt in the dirt to scoop and shift the earth. Making space for the flower they brought from her family's farm in Alabama. A plant passed down and given like a name.

They didn't tame the land, but they watched it. Coddled it. Nurtured it. Making space for the tender-headed moss to thrive, marking off patches where wildflowers would spring. They made a path down past the creek, overlooking the waterfall, up through the trees to the pasture and back down through the trees again. Narrow, winding. Enough space to walk, but barely. The footpath — a compromise like a curfew. Giving the land freedom to grow but still oversight, guidance. A steady hand to help temper the wildness.

Now, when a friend calls to walk the trail with him, someone to talk to and answer back, he tells them "follow me and step where I step." Step where I step so you won't disturb the trees. Step where I step so you won't trample a flower gathering the courage to raise its head and finally break through.

Step where I step. Step where I step and every time the words leave his lips in a frown. With her, they both knew. Always.

Step where I step, the words like wedding vows. Go where I go and I will follow you anywhere.

She still does. They still do. Every day he walks the path, making notes, looking for the first bit of green peeking up through the fallen leaves, listening for the call of the woodthrush, the nut hatch and she is there with him. Always a step ahead or a step behind.

He walks the woods to keep her alive, to keep himself alive, to keep their life alive. He makes meticulous notes. Pages and pages of plans for what happens when he's gone. How the land should be cared for, fostered, encouraged, allowed the freedom to grow and change. Every day he spends hours walking, slowly, but eyes searching with fervor. Fear of missing something — that his land, this land, their land, her legacy and his will be taken for granted, used, trampled, abused. Tamed and torn down. The path through the woods widened for two, then ten until there's no need for a path at all. All the wildflowers gone, forgotten and rotted beneath the soil.

He makes more notes. He finds someone to walk the path with him. Watching as they walk, seeing if they see what he saw, what she saw. An audition to find someone who will listen and remember. A guardian to step in and care for the land and someone he can trust if there is something he did forget. In case he failed to think of every last thing because she would have remembered. She always remembered the details — that the mayapples come early and never last. That the stones in the path wobble after a hard rain making it easy to slip.

Every day, she feels further and further away on their walks. Two steps ahead, then five, ten. He wants to tell her to wait, slow down, but he knows he's the one whose pace is all wrong. Time fading his memory, moments slipping like the Alabama soil from the roots of the family flower they planted so long ago.

He clings to old stories, faded photographs, this land she loved. But every season, every spring, it's harder. The empty space at his side looms larger. The walks are lonelier. The wonder of it all fading further, too. The land they loved more a prison, an anchor keeping him rooted in place. He wants more than anything, to have his work finished, to be able to leave this land.

He says, "don't you wish you knew these things when you were six instead of now, when you are just waiting to die?"

If he had started earlier, he could have finished by now.

If he had pushed his grief aside to find someone to take over, maybe he could have caught up by now. If he had known he would lose her so soon, he would have never walked these woods without her. Not before and not after.

Overlooking the wide expanse of the creek where it Ys and bends, he says "when we moved here, we could step across to the other side and now…" He waves his arm in a cross between wonder at the awesome power of the water to carve and shape but also in the way time widens the distance.

When she first passed, he could smell her, still, in the house. Whispers of jasmine and lilac in the corners of rooms. Close his eyes and hear her laugh. Almost see her doubled over on the creek-side after the bridge failed and he slipped into the stream. How confused he looked when he stood — dripping wet and boots full of water.

Now, he is caught in that place of not knowing if he's remembering or reliving a memory. Like picturing her smile as the one in the photo he keeps in his wallet instead of the myriad of smiles she saved only for him. Mischievous, playful, serious, annoyed. The smirk of being right. The surprise and awe when they saw the first blossom on a stalk, the sunrise between the trees after the leaves fell. The way she would grab him, then, to pull him close. Looping their arms. The way her body folded into his.

And, the sound of his name in her mouth. A simple name, one syllable but bigger, fuller somehow when it came from her. The way she said it when she was happy. When she was excited, frustrated, irritated, curious, angry. The sigh of it when she looked at him starry-eyed. When he knew, felt it in his bones, if nothing else, she loved him almost as much as he loved her.

He knows he knew the difference once. But not now.

Time makes him angry. Bitter. Dries up his mouth like the bite of an apple before it's ready. His painstaking catalog of the land, the stacks of notebooks tracing every flower, every bird through years of springs but not a word about the way she looked at the kitchen sink, suds to her elbows and lost in thought. Nothing written about the way she knelt, hand out and hopeful, to offer corn to the geese in spring.

Does he even remember her at all anymore? The way she was before she was sick? The way she was on a random Tuesday when their life was special and perfect and boring?

Does he remember himself anymore? Strong and sun-tanned before the weight of waiting left him twisted and bent?

Every day, he walks the path and fights the wave of anger that threatens to crest at any moment. To wash away all she worked for because he failed to find someone, the right someone to tend their land. Instead, he keeps walking, watching, making lists. Because for her, he will find someone. Someone willing to learn to step where he stepped, where she stepped. To keep alive her memory, the wildflowers and his.

Charley Allen-Dunn is a poet, web developer, and woodturner. She writes about life, love, loss, and being gay in the South. She earned a degree in creative writing from Murray State University. She and her wife live in far western Kentucky with two dogs and too many cats. *The Scar It Leaves* is her first chapbook.

www.ingramcontent.com/pod-product-compliance
Lightning Source LLC
Chambersburg PA
CBHW030459100426
42813CB00002B/273

9781599246406